Amanda Clarke is a visionary author and mystic who has dedicated her life to unraveling the enigmatic ties that bind the natural world to the spiritual. With an unwavering passion for the animal kingdom and a profound interest in divination, Amanda has crafted "Daily Wisdom: Spirit Animal Oracle," a groundbreaking work that invites readers into the sacred realm of spirit animal guides.

"Daily Wisdom: Spirit Animal Oracle" is more than a book; it's an invitation to forge a deeper connection with the spiritual essences that guide and protect us. Through the vibrant pages of this oracle, Amanda shares her wisdom and insights, offering readers a unique pathway to daily personal growth, enlightenment, and understanding. Each spirit animal is meticulously presented, not just as a symbol, but as a living guide with a daily guidance message vital to our journey.

Amanda Clarke's work is a celebration of the mystical bond between humans and the animal spirits that accompany us. As an ardent advocate for spiritual awakening and the transformative power of mindful living, she encourages readers to open their hearts to the lessons offered by their animal guides. Through "Divine Guidance: Spirit Animal Oracle," Amanda offers a key to unlocking the mysteries of the universe, one spirit animal at a time.

Embark on this enchanting journey with Amanda, and discover the profound wisdom waiting to be revealed by your spirit animal companions.

More on the Bookshelves at www.korupublishing.com

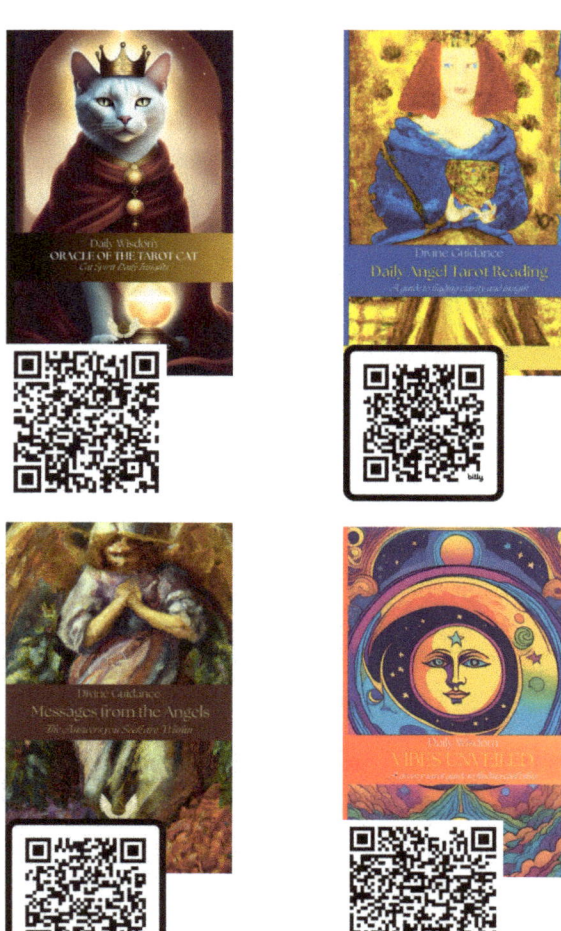

Daily Wisdom
Spirit Animal Oracle
Your Spirit Animal Pocket Companion

Amanda M Clarke

Copyright © 2024 by Koru Lifestylist

All rights reserved. All content, materials, and intellectual property in this book or any other platform owned by Koru Lifestylist are protected by copyright laws. This includes text, images, graphics, videos, audio, software, and any other form of content that may be produced by Koru Lifestylist.

No part of this content may be reproduced, distributed, or transmitted in any form or by any means without the prior written permission of Koru Lifestylist. This means that you cannot copy, reproduce, or use any of the content in this book for commercial or personal purposes without the express written consent of Koru Lifestylist.

Unauthorized use of any copyrighted material owned by Koru Lifestylist may result in legal action being taken against you. Koru Lifestylist reserves the right to pursue all available legal remedies against any individual or entity found to be infringing on its copyright.

In summary, Koru Lifestylist © 2024 holds exclusive rights to all the content produced by it, and any unauthorized use of such content will result in legal action.

My dear beloved seekers of wisdom,

Welcome to a journey where whimsy meets wisdom, guided by the vibrant spirits of the animal kingdom in "Spirit Animal Oracle." This book is your passport to fun, a guide crafted with the sole purpose of sprinkling joy and lightness on the path you walk. As you turn these pages, let laughter be your compass and curiosity your guide, exploring the playful guidance our animal guides generously offer.

Life, in its essence, is meant to be a delightful adventure, easy to navigate and filled with moments of sheer happiness. Sometimes, we forget this simple truth, allowing our minds to become mazes of untold stories and unsung songs. It's time to declutter, to share our stories with the stars, and to find clarity in the wisdom of our furry, feathered, and finned friends.

Howl your worries away with the wolf under the moonlight, soar on life's currents like an eagle, and find the art of living in the present moment as effortlessly as a flamingo stands in contemplation. And the rabbit? Well, let's just say they remind us to embrace the joys of life fully.

Here's to a journey of discovery, laughter, and the wonderful unpredictability of the Spirit Animal kingdom. Have fun, embrace the flow, and remember—life is a playground, and you're here to play.

With joy and a touch of whimsy,

Amanda Clarke

Disclaimer: This Spirit Animal Oracle book provides information on spiritual readings and interpretation, but it is not intended as a substitute for professional advice, diagnosis, or treatment. The information contained in this book is provided for educational and entertainment purposes only and is not meant to be taken as specific advice for individual circumstances. The author and publisher make no representations or warranties with respect to the accuracy or completeness of the contents of this book and specifically disclaim any implied warranties of merchantability or fitness for a particular purpose. The reader should always consult with a licensed professional for any specific concerns or questions. The author and publisher shall not be liable for any loss or damage caused or alleged to have been caused, directly or indirectly, by the information contained in this book. The use of this book is at the reader's sole risk

How to Use "Daily Wisdom: Spirit Animal Oracle"

Welcome to Your Journey of Discovery

"Daily Wisdom: Spirit Animal Oracle" is not just a book; it's a doorway to deeper understanding and connection with the natural and spiritual worlds. This guide will help you navigate its pages, clearing energies and allowing divine guidance to reveal the spirit animal meant to guide you at this moment in your life.

Preparing Your Space

1. Find a Quiet Space: Choose a calm and comfortable spot where you can be undisturbed for a while.
2. Clear the Energy: You may use sage, palo santo, or any other cleansing tool to purify the space around you. Lightly fan the smoke (if using) around yourself and the book, setting the intention to clear any stagnant or negative energies.
3. Set Your Intention: Holding the book in your hands, close your eyes, and take a few deep breaths. Mentally or aloud, state your intention to receive guidance from the spirit animal that most needs to make itself known to you now.

Connecting with Your Spirit Animal

1. Flip Through the Pages: Still holding your intention, gently shuffle through the pages of the book. You can do this by fanning the pages or simply flipping through them without looking.
2. Stop and Discover: When you feel it's the right moment, stop flipping and let your hand choose a page. This is where trust in

the divine guidance comes in—your spirit animal will find you.
3. Reveal and Reflect: Open the book to the page you've selected. The spirit animal on this page is your guide. Take a moment to absorb the image, the name, and the message of the animal.

Delving Deeper

1. Read and Reflect: Spend time reading about your spirit animal. What qualities does it embody? What message is it bringing you? How does it relate to your current situation or the questions you've been pondering?
2. Meditate on the Message: After reading, close your eyes and meditate on the guidance provided. Visualize the spirit animal and ask for any additional insights or clarifications.
3. Journal Your Thoughts: It's beneficial to journal about the insights and feelings that arise. Write down the spirit animal's message, how it applies to your life, and any actions you feel compelled to take. You will find journalling pages at the back of this book.

Integrating the Guidance

1. Act on the Insights: Consider the practical ways you can apply the wisdom and guidance of your spirit animal in your daily life. This might involve changing a habit, making a decision, or seeing a situation from a new perspective.
2. Express Gratitude: Close your session by thanking your spirit animal for the guidance provided. Gratitude strengthens your connection to the spiritual realm and opens your heart to further guidance.

Revisiting

Repeat as Needed: You can return to "Divine Guidance: Spirit Animal Oracle" whenever you seek insight or feel the need for spiritual support. Each interaction can reveal new layers of wisdom and guidance.

Remember, the journey with your spirit animal is deeply personal and unique. Embrace the messages with an open heart and mind, and allow the divine wisdom of the natural world to illuminate your path.

The Answers You Seek

Are Within

Electric Eel

Energy, transformation, intuition

Electric Eels remind us of the importance of channeling our inner energy and intuition for transformation and navigating life's waters.

My Mantra..

I channel transformative energy and intuition, like the Electric Eel, navigating life's currents with power.

Penguin

Adaptability, survival, community

Penguins remind us of the importance of adaptability and the strength found in community and working together towards common goals.

My Mantra..

In community and adaptability, I find my strength

Butterfly

Transformation, grace, freedom

Butterflies symbolize transformation and the graceful acceptance of change, teaching us that growth requires letting go of the past.

My Mantra...

I embrace transformation with grace and freedom.

Eagle

Vision, courage, sovereignty

Eagles inspire us to rise above mundane matters to achieve a higher perspective, encouraging us to embrace courage and sovereignty in our lives.

My Mantra..

My vision and courage guide me to sovereignty.

Deer

Gentleness, intuition, grace

Deer represent gentleness and intuition, reminding us to move through life with grace and to listen to the inner voice for guidance.

My Mantra...

With gentleness and intuition, I navigate life's paths.

Wolf

Intelligence, freedom, social connection

Wolves emphasize the value of intelligence, freedom, and the strength of social connections in navigating the complexities of life.

My Mantra..

Through intelligence and connection, I find my way.

Bear

Strength, solitude, protection

Bears teach us about the power of solitude and introspection for healing and protection, urging us to find strength within ourselves.

My Mantra..

I draw strength from solitude and introspection.

Fox

Cunning, strategy, adaptability

Foxes are known for their cunning and adaptability, showing us the importance of strategy and flexibility in addressing life's challenges.

My Mantra..

Flexibility and cunning pave my road to success.

Hawk

Perspective, spirituality, messages

Hawks offer perspective and spirituality, encouraging us to pay attention to the messages from the universe and our intuition.

My Mantra...

I listen to the universe and trust my intuition.

Rabbit

Abundance, fertility, vulnerability

Rabbits symbolize abundance and fertility, reminding us to embrace opportunities while being mindful of our vulnerabilities.

My Mantra..

I welcome abundance with awareness of my vulnerability.

Turtle

Longevity, endurance, steadiness

Turtles teach us about the virtues of longevity, endurance, and the steady progress towards our goals, emphasizing patience and persistence.

My Mantra...

Patience and persistence guide me towards my goals.

Koala

Reflection, calmness, connection to nature

Koalas remind us to slow down, cherish quiet moments, and deepen our connection with the natural world and our inner selves.

My Mantra..

In stillness, I connect deeply with nature and myself.

Seahorse

Patience, perspective, persistence

Seahorses teach us the power of patience, viewing life from different perspectives, and the importance of persistence in achieving our goals.

My Mantra..

With patience and persistence, I gain new perspectives.

Panther

Courage, leadership, decisiveness

Panthers inspire us to embrace our power, make decisive actions, and lead with courage in the face of darkness and the unknown.

My Mantra..

I lead with courage and decisive action in every step.

Firefly

Illumination, inspiration, hope

Fireflies light up the darkest nights, reminding us that even in darkness, we can find inspiration and hope to guide us forward.

My Mantra...

I find hope and inspiration, lighting up my path.

Otter

Joy, playfulness, family

Otters bring joy and remind us of the importance of play and family connections in nurturing our spirits and fostering relationships.

My Mantra..

In play and family, I find joy and connection.

Walrus

Protection, social connection, adaptability

Walruses encourage us to seek strong social bonds and adapt to the environment, reminding us of the strength found in community.

My Mantra..

Together, we adapt and protect each other.

Woodpecker

Determination, rhythm, communication

Woodpeckers teach us the power of determination and the importance of finding our own rhythm and way of communicating in the world.

My Mantra..

With determination and my unique rhythm, I create my path.

Lynx

Insight, intuition, mystery

The lynx represents the ability to see through deception, encouraging us to trust our intuition and embrace the mysteries of life.

My Mantra...

I trust my intuition and embrace life's mysteries with insight.

Moth

Transformation, hidden knowledge, intuition

Moths remind us of the transformation that comes from following our intuition and seeking the light of hidden knowledge.

My Mantra...

Guided by intuition, I seek the light of transformation.

Porpoise

Intelligence, communication, community

Porpoises symbolize the joy found in effective communication and the strength of community bonds in navigating life's waters.

My Mantra..

In communication and community, I find intelligence and joy.

Frog

Cleansing, renewal, transformation

Frogs remind us to embrace change and cleanse our lives, encouraging personal growth and the shedding of old habits for renewal.

My Mantra..

I embrace renewal and welcome transformation.

Raven

Mystery, magic, intelligence

Ravens inspire us to explore the unknown and find magic in life's mysteries, embracing intelligence and adaptability on our journey.

My Mantra...

I find magic in the mystery and wisdom in the journey.

Shark

Survival, adaptability, instincts

Sharks teach us the power of instincts and survival, urging us to trust our gut feelings and be relentless in our pursuits.

My Mantra..

My instincts guide me through life's waters.

Jaguar

Power, ferocity, the unknown

Jaguars encourage embracing our inner strength and exploring the shadow parts of our spirit, acknowledging the power within the unknown.

My Mantra...

I explore my power and the unknown with courage.

Monkey

Playfulness, curiosity, innovation

Monkeys highlight the importance of playfulness and innovation in solving problems, reminding us to approach life with curiosity.

My Mantra..

Curiosity and playfulness light my path.

Zebra

Individuality, balance, agility

Zebras teach us the value of embracing our uniqueness while finding balance and harmony in the diversity of life.

My Mantra..

I celebrate my uniqueness and seek balance in diversity.

Peacock

Beauty, self-expression, confidence

Peacocks inspire us to show our true colors and find confidence in self-expression, standing out with beauty and grace.

My Mantra...

I express my true self with confidence and grace.

Panda

Peace, balance, gentle strength

Pandas remind us to seek peace and harmony, encouraging gentle strength and balance in our interactions and environment.

My Mantra...

In peace and balance, I find my strength

Giraffe

Perspective, foresight, elegance

Giraffes offer the lesson of looking ahead and seeing beyond the immediate, valuing perspective and foresight in life's journey.

My Mantra..

I look ahead with foresight and perspective.

Crow

Magic, mystery, intelligence

Crows are messengers of magic, urging us to find intelligence and adaptability in navigating life's mysteries and changes.

My Mantra..

I navigate life's mysteries with intelligence and adaptability.

Coyote

Trickster, adaptability, wisdom

Coyotes, the tricksters, remind us to find wisdom in adaptability and to embrace the unexpected turns of life with a light heart.

My Mantra..

I embrace change and wisdom in life's unexpected turns.

Beetle

Rebirth, protection, persistence

Beetles symbolize the resilience and transformation in rebirth, encouraging us to trust in the journey of personal transformation.

My Mantra..

I trust in my journey of transformation and rebirth.

Squirrel

Preparation, activity, balance

Squirrels teach the importance of readiness and gathering resources for the future, emphasizing preparation and balance in life.

My Mantra...

Preparation and balance guide me towards the future.

Bat

Rebirth, intuition, letting go

Bats inspire us to embrace change as a path to growth, letting go of the old to make way for new beginnings and insights.

My Mantra..

I let go of the old and welcome new beginnings.

Swan

Grace, beauty, love

Swans embody elegance and depth of feeling, reminding us to navigate life and relationships with grace, beauty, and love.

My Mantra...

With grace and love, I move through life.

Dragonfly

Change, light, adaptability

Dragonflies say be open to change and let your spirit adapt with agility. The lightness of being will guide you through transitions.

My Mantra..

I embrace change with adaptability and light.

Turtle

Longevity, protection, patience

Turtles embrace the slow and steady path to wisdom. Your resilience and patience afford you protection and longevity.

My Mantra...

My path is protected by patience and resilience.

Hummingbird

Joy, lightness, agility

Hummingbirds seek out the joy in life's small moments. Your agility and lightness uplift those around you, spreading happiness.

My Mantra..

Joy and lightness guide my way through life.

Whale

Wisdom, history, emotional rebirth

Whales dive deep into the emotional depths to find healing and renewal. The wisdom of the ages guides you towards rebirth.

My Mantra..

In depth, I find wisdom and emotional renewal.

Elephant

Strength, loyalty, ancient wisdom

Elephants stand tall in your strength and loyalty. Draw upon ancient wisdom to navigate the present and lead with integrity.

My Mantra..

With strength and wisdom,
I lead and protect.

Horse

Freedom, power, endurance

Horses embrace the journey ahead with the endurance to overcome obstacles. Your freedom is in your power to persevere.

My Mantra...

My power and freedom fuel my journey's endurance.

Lion

Courage, strength, leadership

Lions lead with courage and strength. Your leadership inspires others, drawing from the well of your inner power.

My Mantra..

With courage and strength, I lead and inspire.

Dolphin

Playfulness, intelligence, communication

Dolphins communicate with joy and intelligence. In playfulness, find the depth of connection and understanding with others.

My Mantra..

Through playfulness and intelligence, I connect deeply.

Spider

Creativity, patience, the interweaving of fate

Oh Spider, weave your reality with patience and creativity. Your life's web is intricate, reflecting the beauty of your journey.

My Mantra..

I weave my life's tapestry with creativity and patience.

Snake

Rebirth, transformation, healing

Snakes embrace change as a path to healing. Transformation brings renewal, guiding you to your next stage of growth.

My Mantra...

In transformation, I find healing and rebirth.

Deer

Gentleness, sensitivity, peace

Deer moves through life with grace and gentleness. Be sensitive to the feelings of others, finding peace in your surroundings.

My Mantra...

I move with gentleness and seek peace in every step.

Owl

Wisdom, intuition, the ability to see what others do not

Owl says trust in your wisdom and intuition. Look beyond the surface to see deeper truths others may miss.

My Mantra..

My intuition guides me to unseen truths.

Tiger

Power, passion, unpredictability

Be a Tiger, embrace your inner power and passion. Let your presence be known, but be mindful of the unpredictability of life.

My Mantra..

I embrace my power and passion with a mindful heart.

Rabbit

Abundance, comfort, vulnerability

Rabbits welcome abundance and seek comfort in the small joys. Remember, vulnerability is not a weakness, but a strength.

My Mantra..

I find strength in my vulnerability and joy in abundance.

Hawk

Perspective, spirituality, focus

Hawk says takes a moment to gain perspective on your situation. A broader view will bring clarity and focus to your spiritual journey.

My Mantra..

From a higher perspective,
I find focus and clarity.

Wolf

Intuition, freedom, social connections

Wolf says trust your instincts and seek connections with others. Embrace your freedom to explore the world around you.

My Mantra..

I trust my intuition and embrace freedom.

Bear

Strength, confidence, healing

Bear spirit says believe in your own power and strength. Healing comes from within, so give yourself time and space to mend.

My Mantra..

I am strong, confident, and in a state of healing.

Fox

Cleverness, adaptability, discretion

Just like a Fox use your wits and adaptability to navigate through life. Be discreet in your actions and choose your paths wisely.

My Mantra..

My cleverness guides me through life's twists and turns.

Butterfly

Transformation, grace, change
acceptance

The Butterfly embraces change with grace. Let go of the old to make room for the new and transform your life.

My Mantra..

I gracefully accept and embrace transformation.

Eagle

Vision, freedom, authority

The Eagle see's the bigger picture and rises above the mundane. Your vision will guide you to freedom and authority in your life.

My Mantra...

My vision guides me to soar above challenges.

Dove

Peace, love, guidance

Doves bring messages of peace and love, reminding us to stay calm and centered and to spread kindness wherever we go.

My Mantra...

I embrace peace and love, guided by the gentle spirit of the Dove.

Salmon

Determination, change, resilience

Salmon inspire us with their determination to swim upstream, symbolizing the resilience needed to face life's challenges and embrace change.

My Mantra..

With the resilience of the Salmon, I face challenges head-on, embracing change.

Flamingo

Balance, community, individuality

Flamingos encourage us to maintain balance in our lives while celebrating our individuality within the context of a larger community.

My Mantra...

I find balance and celebrate my individuality, inspired by the Flamingo's grace.

Bee

Community, brightness, personal power

Bees remind us of the importance of community and working together towards a common goal while embracing our personal power.

My Mantra...

I embrace community and personal power, inspired by the Bee.

Crane

Longevity, balance, grace

Cranes symbolize grace and balance in our lives, teaching us the value of staying grounded while also aspiring for higher wisdom.

My Mantra...

With grace and balance, I aspire for wisdom, guided by the Crane.

Elk

Stamina, strength, agility

Elk represent strength and endurance, encouraging us to pace ourselves and use our energy wisely to overcome obstacles.

My Mantra...

I harness strength and endurance, walking the path of the Elk.

Goldfish

Abundance, harmony, luck

Goldfish are symbols of abundance and harmony, reminding us that luck often comes to those who are patient and observant.

My Mantra..

In harmony and patience, I attract abundance, like the Goldfish.

Iguana

Adaptability, survival, perception

Iguanas teach us the value of adaptability and the importance of blending in or standing out as the situation requires for survival.

My Mantra...

Adaptability guides me through life's challenges, with the spirit of the Iguana.

Monkey

Curiosity, playfulness, intelligence

Monkeys inspire curiosity and a playful approach to life, reminding us that intelligence and innovation come from exploring our world.

My Mantra...

Curiosity and playfulness enrich my journey, enlightened by the Monkey.

Quail

Courage, protection, group harmony

Quails embody courage and the strength found in numbers, urging us to protect those in our community and find harmony in our group.

My Mantra..

In courage and unity, I find strength, following the Quail's example.

Pelican

Generosity, abundance, patience

Pelicans are symbols of generosity and patience, teaching us the importance of giving to others and waiting for the right moment.

My Mantra..

Generosity and patience fill my heart, embodying the Pelican's spirit.

Unicorn

Purity, magic, possibility

Unicorns remind us of the magic in believing in possibilities and the purity of our intentions in seeking out the goodness in the world.

My Mantra...

I believe in magic and possibility, walking in the light of the Unicorn.

Vulture

Renewal, patience, transformation

Vultures teach us the importance of renewal and the transformation that comes with patience and understanding.

My Mantra...

I embrace transformation with patience and understanding, guided by the Vulture.

Wombat

Persistence, courage, resourcefulness

Wombats remind us of the power of persistence and courage, utilizing our resourcefulness to navigate challenges.

My Mantra..

Persistence and courage shape my path, inspired by the Wombat.

Xerus

Resourcefulness, survival, community

Xerus (African ground squirrels) symbolize the strength found in community and the ability to survive through resourcefulness.

My Mantra..

In community and resourcefulness, I find survival, like the Xerus.

Yak

Strength, resilience, adaptability

Yaks encourage us to embrace our strength and resilience, adapting to harsh conditions with steadfast determination.

My Mantra..

My resilience adapts to all conditions, embodying the spirit of the Yak.

Angelfish

Grace, beauty, serenity

Angelfish inspire grace and serenity, reminding us to move through life with beauty and a calm demeanor.

My Mantra..

Grace and serenity flow through me, mirrored in the Angelfish.

Condor

Freedom, vision, leadership

Condors represent freedom and the ability to see the bigger picture, leading with vision and high perspective.

My Mantra..

I lead with vision, soaring to new heights like the Condor.

Bobcat

Adaptability, independence, mystery

Bobcats teach us the value of adaptability and the mystery of walking our path with independence and confidence.

My Mantra..

Adaptability and mystery define my journey, following the Bobcat.

Dingo

Adaptability, resourcefulness, endurance

Dingoes remind us of the importance of endurance and resourcefulness, thriving in various environments through adaptability.

My Mantra...

Endurance and resourcefulness are my strengths, learned from the Dingo.

Gazelle

Agility, beauty, speed

Gazelles embody agility and speed, teaching us to move gracefully and swiftly, embracing the beauty of motion.

My Mantra..

I move through life with agility and grace, capturing the essence of the Gazelle.

Hyena

Strategy, intelligence, adaptability

Hyenas highlight the strategy and intelligence required to adapt and thrive in a competitive world.

Strategy and intelligence guide my adaptations, channeling the Hyena.

Impala

Agility, awareness, grace

Impalas remind us of the importance of agility and awareness, gracefully navigating life's challenges.

My Mantra...

Awareness and agility navigate me through life, reflecting the Impala.

Jackal

Intelligence, adaptability, perception

Jackals bring the wisdom of adaptability and perception, understanding the environment to make informed decisions.

My Mantra..

I perceive and adapt with intelligence, drawing wisdom from the Jackal.

Tuna

Speed, endurance, strength

Tunas symbolize the strength and endurance needed to traverse great distances, harnessing the power of speed.

My Mantra..

Speed and strength carry me far, embracing the endurance of the Tuna.

My Journaling Pages

My daily thoughts....

My daily thoughts....

My daily thoughts....

My daily thoughts....

My daily thoughts....

My daily thoughts....

My daily thoughts....

My daily thoughts....

My daily thoughts....

My daily thoughts....

My daily thoughts....

My daily thoughts....

My daily thoughts....

My daily thoughts....

My daily thoughts....

My daily thoughts....

My daily thoughts....

My daily thoughts....

My daily thoughts....

My daily thoughts....

My daily thoughts....

My daily thoughts....

www.ingramcontent.com/pod-product-compliance
Lightning Source LLC
Chambersburg PA
CBHW042342300426
44109CB00048B/2625